TITLES AVAILABLE IN THIS AND OTHER...

On this and the following page is a full list of titles in our TQM Practitioner Series, Business ...
Practitioner Series and our new Business Performance Improvement Practitioner Series. Some reviews of individual
titles are included below.

> '...one of the best (reports) yet encountered.'
> *Automotive Engineer*

> '...a welcome contribution with lots of useful and clearly written information and guidance.'
> *Integrated Environmental Management*

> '...clearly written...useful for anyone in business.'
> *Waste and Water Treatment*

Details of where to get further information can be found overleaf.

Title	ISBN	Price (£)
TQM Practitioner Series		
TQM – The Hands-On Experience: People Make Quality	0 7487 1845 1	29.50
Forms and Other Documents for Use in BS EN ISO 9000 Quality Systems	0 7487 1846 X	29.50
Essential TQM Tools and Techniques: A Practical Business Handbook	0 7487 1847 8	29.50
Gaining and Benefiting from ISO 9000 Registration: A Step-by-step Guide (Second Edition)	0 7487 1837 0	29.50
A Quality Auditing Manual (Second Edition)	0 7487 1840 0	29.50
Sustaining Quality Advantage in Financial Services	0 7487 1828 1	35.00
Beyond the BS 5750/ISO 9000 Certificate: The Bureaucracy Buster's Guide to Quality Assurance	0 7487 2106 1	29.50
Writing an ISO 9000 Quality Manual: Practical Guidelines	0 946655 89 8	29.50
Risk Management in a TQM Environment	0 7487 1905 9	29.50
FMEAs: A Manager's Handbook	0 7487 1861 3	29.50
TQM: Its Impact on Bottom Line Results	0 946655 96 0	29.50
The Role of Junior and Middle Level Management in TQM	0 946655 74 X	29.50
Quality Function Deployment	0 946655 72 3	29.50
The Role of the Modern Quality Manager	0 7487 1867 2	29.50
Measuring Service Quality	0 946655 75 8	29.50
TQM in Sales and Marketing	0 946655 76 6	29.50
TQM: Does It Always Work?	0 7487 1936 9	29.50
Communication in Successful TQM	0 7487 1872 9	29.50
Kaizen	0 7487 1901 6	29.50
TQM Training	0 7487 1871 0	29.50
Teams and TQM	0 7487 1870 2	29.50
QA and ISO 9000/BS 5750 in the Hospitality and Catering Industries	0 7487 1869 9	35.00
BS 7750: What the New Environmental Management Standard Means for your Business	0 946655 60 X	29.50
TQM in Service Industries: A Practitioner's Manual	0 7487 1914 8	29.50
Managing and Improving Service Quality and Delivery	0 7487 1907 5	29.50
Competitive Benchmarking: An Executive Guide	0 7487 1926 1	29.50
TQM-Based Performance Measurement: Practical Guidelines	0 946655 52 9	29.50
Quality Costs: Their Impact on Company Strategy and Profitability	0 7487 1875 3	29.50
Customer Care: Strategy for the 90s	0 7487 1868 0	29.50
Ensuring Your Business Achieves and Profits from BS 5750 Registration: A Practical Guide	0 946655 44 8	29.50
Leadership of Customer-Driven TQM	0 7487 1865 6	29.50
TQM in the Electronics Industry: A User's and Supplier's Guide	0 7487 1874 5	29.50
Software Quality Assurance: What It Buys You and What It Costs You	0 7487 1902 4	35.00
Implementing TQM in Small and Medium-Sized Companies	0 946655 59 6	29.50
Selling Professional Services	0 7487 1873 7	29.50

Continued overleaf

If you would like further information, please contact us at the address below. Many companies buy bulk copies of our reports; if you are interested in doing this, we would be pleased to discuss discount levels.

Customer Services Department
Stanley Thornes (Publishers) Limited
Ellenborough House
Wellington Street
CHELTENHAM
Glos. GL50 1YD

Telephone: (01242) 228586
Fax: (01242) 221914

KAIZEN

THE UNDERSTANDING AND APPLICATION OF CONTINUOUS IMPROVEMENT

F. Huda

TQM PRACTITIONER SERIES

SERIES EDITOR: DR M. ZAIRI
THE EUROPEAN CENTRE FOR TQM

STANLEY THORNES

First published by Technical Communications (Publishing) Ltd.

Reprinted in 1994 by:
Stanley Thornes (Publishers) Ltd
Ellenborough House
Wellington Street
CHELTENHAM
Glos. GL50 1YD
United Kingdom

Reprinted 1995

A catalogue record for this book is available from The British Library.

ISBN 0 7487 1901 6

Printed and bound in Great Britain by CIP, Basildon, Essex

Chapter One

INTRODUCTION

Chapter Two

THE BUILDING BLOCKS OF KAIZEN

What is the Kaizen Principle?

Chapter Three

THE PRACTICAL APPLICATION OF KAIZEN

Where can the principles be incorporated ?

Chapter Four

MAN, MACHINES, METHODS, MATERIALS, MEASUREMENT..........36

Chapter Five

WHAT ARE THE COSTS?...52

CASE STUDIES

KAIZEN:

THE UNDERSTANDING AND APPLICATION OF

CONTINUOUS IMPROVEMENT

Note:

In the interests of clarity, the masculine pronoun has been used throughout the text. This is in no way calculated to give offence to female readers, especially since I am one myself !

FAHMIA HUDA, UNIVERSITY OF WESTMINSTER.   1ST SEPTEMBER 1992

Chapter One

INTRODUCTION

Over a period of forty years Japan has become the second largest economy in the world, the third largest trader and the world's largest capital exporter. Fundamental to this volte face has been a move from an agrarian economy to an industrial one, within the confines of societal norms. The fascination of Western managers with the Japanese miracle is teamed with cynicism - suggesting that because their cultural values are different, the same methods employed in the West's environment, wholly geared to individualism, WOULD FAIL.

The aim of this management report is to suggest otherwise. The phenomenon of Kaizen is based on principles which are universal and ubiquitous. They are to be found within every individual, and in every society, such that, arguably, Kaizen could be considered as a bridge between nations rather than as a divisive element.

The initial objective, then, is to understand what Kaizen is, and relate it specifically to its relevance in Western management. As such, the preliminary part of the discussion focuses on the cultural factors which influence it, so that later the implications of cultural diversity can be examined.

The cultural antecedent of Kaizen

First of all, an attempt at a definition: Kaizen translates roughly as the Japanese word for CONTINUOUS IMPROVEMENT.

The concept, however, is of *gradual* change, of ongoing, unnoticeable improvements which aggregate over a period of time to provide visible proof that things are getting better.

This is in contrast to that other kind of change called INNOVATION, with which the West is more readily associated. It is abrupt, upheaving, chaotic and usually relates to the short-term.

Kaizen is more complex in that it encompasses a multitude of different ideas ranging from total quality control to employee involvement. It is also simple because it focuses on getting back to basics. The contrast with the West is provided in that Kaizen puts people first, rather than concentrating on profit

2

margins and other financially related topics. This not to say that profits are not important in the overall context, but they are brought about by different management methods which do not involve conflict.

Instead of a results-oriented way of thinking, Kaizen is about process-orientation. By getting the processes right, other things fall into place automatically. This seems to be where the unresolved dichotomy of Japanese and Western business practices lies (never mind the process, where are the profits?).

To understand the influence of cultural norms, one must first answer the question "What is culture?"

Culture is a set of values and social norms which are transmitted from generation to generation and constitute an unwritten code to regulate the behaviour of a group of people.

Central to the idea of Japanese culture is the ideology of 'Japaneseness', a homogeneity of thought and deed on behalf of all the population which seeks to exclude anything foreign as "alien". Such rationalisation based on homogeneity could be construed as a universal panacea to explain all the differences existing between the Orient and the West - characteristics such as submerging of individuality, devotion to the company, co-operation with authority, groupism.

Yet one could argue that many of these same characteristics are apparent in other nations besides Japan, so by default, the argument that Kaizen is culture-bound becomes groundless. Not only that, but such traits are an effect of conditioning rather than inheritance, so where they are weak, they can be strengthened. Kaizen, undiluted, may not be wholly successful in the West, but adapted to co-exist with individualism, it could prove potent indeed.

Some of the practices are already being incorporated into organisations here (for instance, see the Nissan case study) with remarkable results; it is merely that a more holistic approach should be adopted in order to reap later benefits.

The transportability of Kaizen

Technique, technology and innovation have all crossed cultural and international boundaries without reserve; but the same openness to borrowing of ideas in terms of human resources meets constant and unchanging prejudice. But rather than polarising East-West differences, it is more pertinent to

3

concentrate on similarities.

Difficulties in the past have centred around the question of individualism and its inextricable importance in the psychology of work. In Japan, the lowest common denominator is 'WE', whereas in the West it is 'I'. But the work ethic is remarkably similar: the Protestant Work Ethic upon which the West revolves bears resemblance to the code of BUSHIDO (the way of the warrior) and its teachings of frugality, forbearance, hard work and loyalty. Can one really argue that these characteristics do not exist in the West?

The way forward is neither to ignore the importance of WE, nor to sublimate the I. Kaizen can be transplanted more easily into the current philosophy of change, which is less stridently brash than a decade ago. Gentle reversal of policy on building blocks such as motivation, leadership, and communication will open channels that have hitherto remained closed. Competitiveness is there for the taking.

Emphasis should be placed on the group, and this can be geared into practice at the earliest stage. The education system requires a radical re-think to point out the benefits of groupism, whilst allowing scope for an individual to realise his or her maximum potential. Perhaps the greatest influence of the group exists when each individual is taken account of and no-one's position is undermined. This, then, is the central theme to adapting Kaizen to the West: take care of the individuals within each group, then take care of the groups and we have a working methodology for adopting Kaizen into an environment where it can flourish.

Group influences are powerful phenomena and are prevalent throughout the life of an individual. How easy it becomes to mould the working group into an homogeneous whole, with homogeneity being provided by commitment to and participation in an overall visible, achievable goal. Certainly there will remain those whose pioneer spirit must conquer all, but given the choice, how many would work against, instead of with, each other?

The importance of quality and quality control

There is an innate willingness in the Japanese to synthesize the best of what is available and to assimilate it into the fabric of a carefully woven strategy: that strategy is quality.

Quality is of fundamental importance to Kaizen because it means standing back and reappraising in order to do better. Without a conscious effort to introduce

quality into work practices, the concept of continuous improvement becomes meaningless.

The three main objectives of Kaizen which have to be tackled are:

• managerial practices, which must broaden its perspective, whilst increasing its involvement
• shifting values which are socially and culturally adrift as far as quality is concerned
• organisational effectiveness - the aforementioned agenda of leadership, motivation and goal-setting.

Quality means a major rehaul of attitudes is required and the learning experience associated with this is painful, because it means upturning established patterns of behaviour. Working towards introducing quality has to be a rational decision adopted by each employee. This can therefore be seen as a collective consciousness-raising exercise advocating the benefits, whilst highlighting the losses that lack of quality can bring. And when the going gets tough, just think of the ultimate rewards!

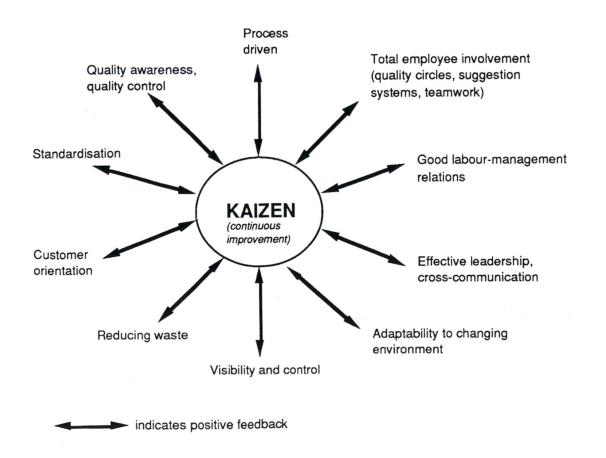

Chapter Two

THE BUILDING BLOCKS OF KAIZEN

What is the Kaizen principle?

• Kaizen is more an amalgam of interrelated principles which singly become trivial, but combined represents a powerful tool for improvement.

• It is an holistic approach to problem solving and is people-based.

• It is a way of providing quality through attention to detail.

Customer focus

There are two types of customer:

• internal to the company, between one employee and another and between one department and another.

• external to the company, which may be singular or plural.

In Kaizen the focus for improvement is in the relationship between the customer and the supplier. The customer is regarded as the beginning and the end point for any drive towards product and service design and delivery.

In any lifecycle, the usual steps are:

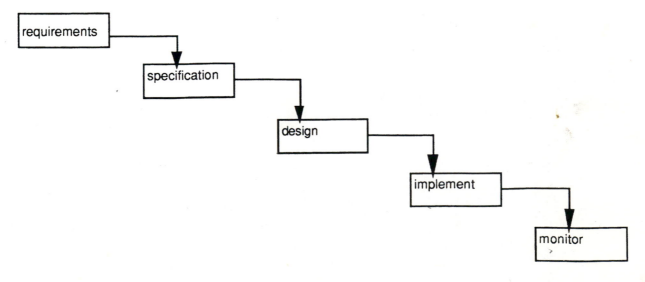

But _who_ determines the requirements? Is there a user-centred approach? Regrettably, the chorus of the majority is NO! Consider a refocus on objectives, which makes this top-down, linear approach more pragmatic, more functional, more geared to the user. More continuous improvement rather than a one-off success or a one-off failure. The result is the PLAN-DO-CHECK-ACTION cycle which is illustrated below.

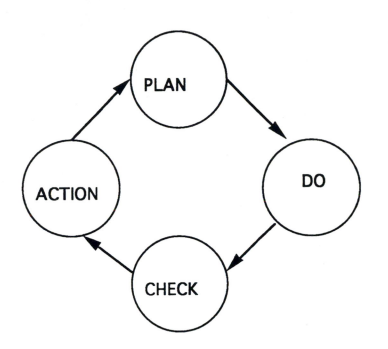

The PDCA cycle

• At the requirements stage, the customer is given priority.

• He is asked for his needs/wants, so that they can be incorporated at this initial stage.

• Only when it has been determined what it is that the customer is demanding from the business (going round the PDCA cycle) does the next phase come into operation.

• A specification is detailed, then designed and finally implemented. There is

scope to return constantly to the documented requirements, indeed to the customers themselves, to ensure that the requirements have been met.

• This focuses the design by doing it right-first-time, so that re-design at a later stage does not become necessary because the organisation has become divorced from the actual needs of its customer.

• The revised lifecycle then becomes:

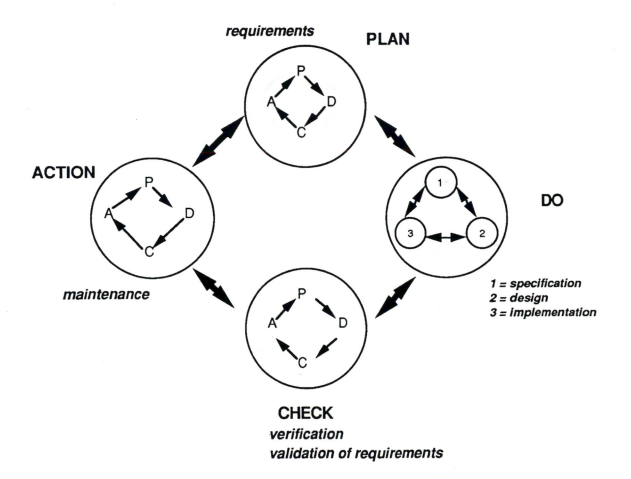

The PDCA cycle is an invaluable tool for management because it allows attention to be focused on the job in hand and also simultaneously for forward planning. Its robustness means that once each stage has been accomplished, tasks are assignable to individuals. This also helps to encourage ownership and responsibility, so that task failure is less likely.

PDCA is ubiqiutous within the Kaizen framework.

• It can be used for data gathering through use of the Seven Statistical Tools (these are discussed later)

• For formulating the best way to implement improvements

• And to measure the extent to which improvement has occurred

• Then to introduce a new standard which provides a reference point for the next phase of improvement

Continuous Improvement rather than innovation

Innovation is equivalent to the great-leap-forward. It is abrupt, challenging, dramatic. It is rarely long-lasting. The ephemeral nature of innovation is comparable to building a sandcastle - glorious for the moment, greatly applauded, but unable to stand the ravages of time and tide.

Kaizen, in comparison, thrives in an atmosphere of stability, because of the strong inherent foundations that already exist and which can be relied upon as a basis for improvement.

Innovation is a creative experience because it can inject freshness into stagnant areas, but by itself, it becomes a house of straw. Vast injections of cash and technology are no substitute to altering behaviour and ideals in the minds of the employees. Only the latter can ensure long-term growth, because they *maintain* the momentum for change. Innovation steadily deteriorates over time unless the implication of changes are amended, maintained, improved. According to Masaaki Imai, there is no such thing as a static constant.

Thus innovation must be succeeded by a Kaizen strategy, if the effects of that great-leap-forward are to be compounded into some solid long-term objectives. (See graph of Kaizen and Innovation comparisons over time).

A Comparison of Innovation and Kaizen

INNOVATION	KAIZEN
Creativity	Adaptability
Individualism	Teamwork, systems-approach
Specialist-oriented	Generalist-oriented
Technology-oriented	People-oriented
Information: closed	Information: open, shared

and proprietory

Functional orientation	Cross-functional orientation
Seeks new technology	Building on existing technology
Limited feedback	Comprehensive feedback

Source: M. Imai,1986

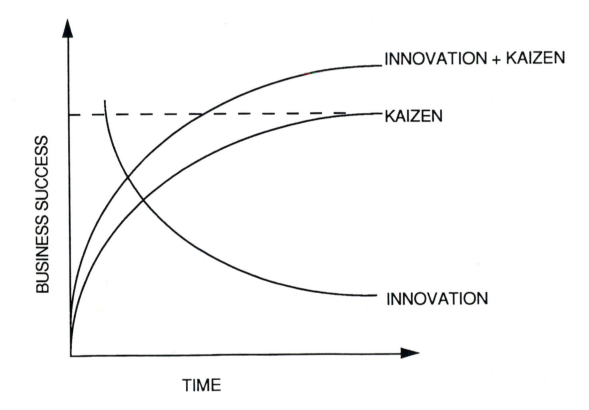

Process-driven not results driven

By focusing on processes, effort is rewarded as much as the ultimate outcome. A further by-product of this is that in getting the process under control, results are automatically improved.

Obsession with results, the 'get-rich-quick' and 'I want it done yesterday, I don't care how!' philosophy are alien to the Kaizen culture. Management loses sight of establishing good working practices, of employee motivation and the

value of each individual's contribution.

Let us see the outcome of results-driven criteria:

• Short-term focus on profit

• Unhappy employees responding to carrot-and-stick mentality

• Lack of individual motivation, therefore frustration with the job

• Absenteeism and high rates of staff turnover

• Tense workplace atmosphere, breakdown in communication between management and employees

• Only achievement is rewarded.

How can process-driven criteria contribute to continuous improvement?

• Restores pride in work

• Processes (i.e., what is actually happening to produce the end-result) are the areas for in-depth analysis. Improving the process automatically ensures that results will be improved.

• Working standards are present

• Invokes discipline, participation, involvement, morale, communication

• Effort and achievement are both rewarded

The next process is the customer

This was a phrase coined by Kaoru Ishikawa (the Father of Total Quality Control) to pave the way for breaking down departmental barriers and promoting cross-functional management.

If quality is to be maintained and improved in the production process, there must be smooth communication between the various people involved in the stages of production and consumption. Thus, the customer can be either the internal customer or the external one, but the principle remains the same:

DON'T PASS ON DEFECTIVE WORK TO THE NEXT PERSON DOWN THE LINE.

This is an absolute criterion of continuous improvement, because a person cannot endlessly firefight against the incompetence or negligence of others. The result would be a chaos of wastage - in time, in money and in people; ultimately in the product itself. Kaizen cannot accommodate waste.

Thus refocusing one's objectives so that sectionalism is reduced within an organisation means that cohesion can be fostered.

Where the external customer is concerned, the concept of 'market-in' not 'product-out' is introduced. This means that it is the influence of the external customer and his perspectives which drive the change, rather than the company creating a product which moulds inadequately to customer needs. The customer becomes the focus for initiating improvement, which is a fundamental axiom for introducing quality into the organisation.

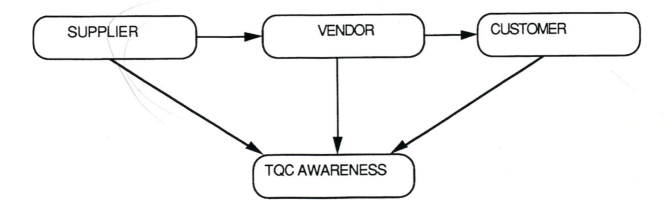

Standardisation

Standardisation is an important part of Kaizen activity because unless standards have been set, there will be no focus for improvement. Following on from the PDCA cycle, the SDCA (Standardise-Do-Check-Action) cycle is brought into play to create a precise form of measurement against which the individual can compare his work. At the same time, having a set of rules to follow challenges his imagination to be able to improve upon those standards and provides the database upon which measurements proceed.

Outcomes of standardisation include:

• enforces discipline on the workforce

• creates greater conformity of output

• can be used as a performance measure which, when combined with the PDCA cycle, allows evaluation of how effective any improvement has been.

One of the chief merits of initiating a Kaizen programme is that it prompts management to ponder whether current standards are present, when they were last appraised and revised, how to challenge them further, even to question why they are needed. Current practices can be scrutinised for shortfall.

How does one go about creating standards? Currently, the British Standard BS 5750 provides general guidelines on establishing a general framework, but in Kaizen, the way forward is to:

• first discover your processes, that is, find out just what it is that you are doing

• find out performance measures, i.e., outputs and inputs, the level at which things are currently being done

• if no standards are in place, then use these as your current levels

• find out ways in which the output can be improved

• initiate improvements and achieve higher standards, which can then be used as the next point of reference for further improvements.

Reducing waste

Waste can be a subtle form of loss or it can be a major haemorrhage depending on how inefficiently an organisation is run. Even before continuous improvement can begin, the problem of waste has to be addressed. Factors such as quality, cost and scheduling are all areas in which waste can occur, but the human factor is no less important. Waste of resources, of talent, is probably the most self-destructive of all.

In order to reduce waste, one must first identify it. The most common checkpoints are listed below:

1. Waste of manpower through inadequate training and development (MAN).

2. Waste in the way that things are done: non-value-adding tasks (METHODS).

3. Waste in unused or underutilised machinery; waste of the machinery if it is not properly maintained (MACHINES).

4. Waste in materials, from paper and other stationery, to waste of raw materials through inventory and stockpiling. Waste when goods have to be warehoused, waste when these deteriorate over time (MATERIALS).

5. General waste through lack of measurements, thus being unaware whether targets are arbitrary or not (MEASUREMENT).

6. Finally, waste in each phase of the work-in-progress, when quality has not been built in, but relies on being inspected out.

To eliminate as much waste as possible, management needs to take a good look at the ways in which current productivity as well as the product itself is being handled. General tightening up of the work-in-progress to produce shorter, better, more 'tuned-in' processes, with a concomitant urgency to do away with unnecessary items like tools, machinery, paper-passing, is very much in line with Kaizen thinking. This will also help with reducing rejects, as well as reducing inventory.

Other ways which can contribute towards waste-consciousness (which can be either physical, emotional or psychological) involve attention to detail and are discussed below.

Getting things right the first time

As has been discussed, the only way in which to achieve right first time is to involve the customer in the equation. Waste is reduced by adhering closely to the customer requirements and designing the product or service within the specifications. This will result in:

less rejects,

in less rework,

and ultimately will save on inspection.

Inspection will then concentrate on the N=2 principle: only the first and the last items of a batch are inspected. If the process has stayed true, these will fall within the control limits and further inspection is not necessary. If, however, they fall outside of the limits, the process is examined for ways in which it has failed and then been recalibrated. It is necessary to treat the source and not the symptoms. No firefighting is allowed in Kaizen. The ultimate aim is to eliminate inspection altogether - zero defects, which will be discussed later.

How can all this be done? The solution is to involve the employee - motivate him, train him, make him problem-conscious, give him ownership on a local as well as on a global level. When responsibility is assumed for that part of the process in which he participates as well as an understanding of its relevance to the wider goals, then right-first-time will be the accepted norm. Pride in workmanship will be restored, and reward and recognition will provide fuel for the restoration to continue.

Poka-Yoke and Zero defects

Inspections are customary in many areas of industry. They are costly, painstaking and eventually, they do not contribute greatly to reducing the error rate in production. The problem is addressed after it has arisen - even 100% inspection will not mean that defectives are rooted out from the system.

The real way to address the problem of error - and error will arise, because that is natural- is to try and eliminate it at the outset. Hence the concept of *poka-yoke*, or mistake-proofing. In reality, the method is very simple: the idea is to identify areas in which errors are likely to occur, then introduce a number of devices which are a fail-safe mechanism for preventing the error in the first place. This ties in with the theme of Kaizen which advocates prevention rather than cure.

Defects are not tolerated, nor are defectives passed down to the next person dealing with the product. Thus, instead of sampling and all its itinerant inaccuracies, self-inspection is promoted, and following that, the person next in the receiving line also checks the item before working on it. This is a dual method for eliminating the inspection role from people who are not directly responsible for the manufacture of the item, and instead passing on the responsibility and ownership for it, to the people concerned.

Zero defects are achieved via a multiplicity of means:

• Source inspection which concentrates on the cause of error, not the effect.

• 100% inspection using mistake-proofing devices.

• Immediate action to stop the mistake from continuing further into the system.

The usefulness of Poka-yoke lies in that it reduces waste - in time, due to less rework, in materials due to less scrap being produced, and in manpower, as more time is spent productively. This is also a motivator for the employee because work becomes pro-active rather than reactive in nature. Some of the ways in which poka-yoke is demonstrated are:

• Guide pins

• Alarms

• Limit switches

• Counters

• Checklists

Errors and defects

Errors cause defects. These can be in two states:

1. About to occur

2. Already occurred

Of course, the logical beginning to this would be to question why errors arise in the first place. The figure overleaf lists some of the more common causes. As can be seen, the majority of error lies with human fallibility.

WHY DO ERRORS ARISE ?

1. HUMAN ERROR
   forgetfulness
   misunderstanding
   wrong identification
   inexperience
   absent-mindedness
   ignoring rules
   delay
   standards unavailable
   surprises due to malfunction
   sabotage
2. MACHINE ERRORS
3. METHODS USED
4. MATERIALS
5. INFORMATION (or lack of it)

In order to remove the defect, there has to be a warning, for example a bell or a buzzer, followed by shutdown of the process which caused the error. This gives a uniform control to the process and allows the error to be dealt with at source. Some machines function automatically in the event of defect, and shutdown automatically. Others require manual control. All require vigilance on the part of the operator, who is the lynchpin for the process.

It must be pointed out that Poka-yoke, as with all the other Kaizen techniques, cannot function in isolation. It requires the participation of all the employees within the company. The will to succeed to prevent errors and therefore the defects that they cause must be adopted unanimously. The benefits, as usual, are potentially enormous.

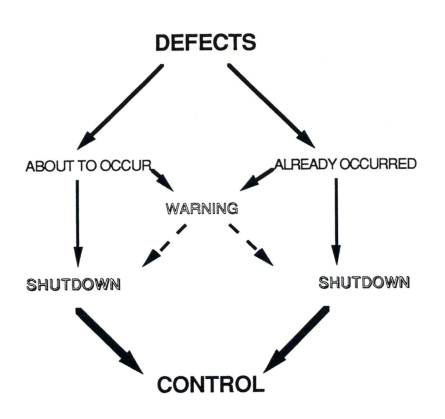

Jidohka

Jidohka or AUTONOMATION is a method initiated by Taichii Ohno at Toyota regarding the production of defects. In order to reduce the amount of waste that occurred, machines were designed to stop automatically whenever a problem arose. Recurrence of the same mistake is then prevented by a thorough check of components, asking the question *'why ?'* enough times to be able to treat the real problem and not the symptoms masking it.

In this way many machines can be looked after by one employee. Furthermore, it reduces checking and maintenance of the machines because they only function when they are producing correct items.

Just-in-time

Consider a factory, for argument's sake, although the discussion is universally applicable.

What are the steps that occur to manufacture a good ?

Purchase and storage

1. Raw materials (stock) are ordered.

2. Additional buffer stock is ordered (just-in-case)

3. This has to be stored, accounted for, delivered as and when necessary

Production

4. The raw materials join the assembly line

5. Scheduling of activities to use those materials

6. Goods may or may not be produced right first time

7. The finished product must be stored, during which time it may have been damaged or has deteriorated in some way, thus becoming unusable.

Delivery

8. Eventually the good is delivered to the consumer

9. This may or may not be the correct item requested.

THE COST OF PRODUCTION AND OVER-PRODUCTION WITHOUT JUST-IN- TIME

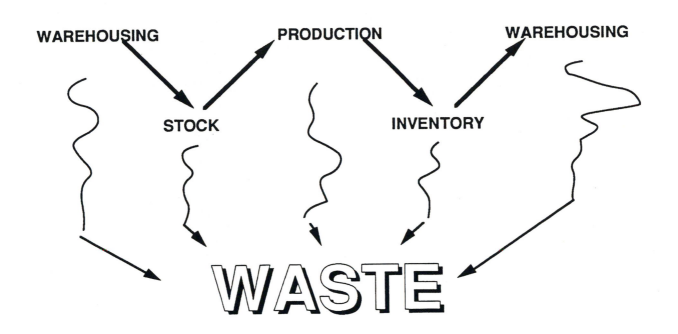

The Just-in-Time philosophy revolves around the elimination of waste and seeks to:
• reduce lot size
• reduce inventory
• reduce scrap and rework

How does it approach the practicalities of these aspirations?

• Firstly, by tightening the processes that go into making a product

• Secondly, by streamlining the flow along the assembly line so that there is neither too much nor too little being produced at each step along the way. The employee and the process are not idle, but they are also not overwhelmed.

• Thirdly, by overlapping operations

• Fourthly, by minimising set-up times

• Fifthly, by actively involving the employee

The end result is PIECE-FOR-PIECE PROCESSING. No storage, no buffer stocks, no damage, no waste. **No Worries.**

Chapter Three

THE PRACTICAL APPLICATION OF KAIZEN

Where can the principles be incorporated?

According to Masaaki Imai, there are three areas in which Kaizen can be implemented. These are:

• management level
• group level
• individual level

Breakdown of Kaizen responsibility and awareness into these entities means that each group of people has a specific set of tasks to achieve to contribute towards the overall goal of continuous improvement. One must also consider the 'big picture', i.e., the organisation and its particular culture, as this is of paramount importance when trying to effect change. No matter how well each individual or set of individuals work, if the organisation is not geared to nurturing their efforts, these efforts will have been in vain. Precedence, then, should be given to looking at the organisation.

At the organisational level

Harmonious industrial relations

Kaizen is interested in co-operation rather than confrontation. Management and unions need to work together in harmony for their mutual benefit: the unions to achieve job security and healthy remuneration for their members; management to ensure satisfied workers who can attend to their task instead of squabbling about pay and conditions. This requires flexibility and consensus from both parties, the admission that problems do exist and a concerted attitude of unity towards solving them.

Psychological barriers to harmonious labour-management relations are the real hurdles to be overcome in order to achieve communication between labour and management. The way to set about reducing conflict is to make *all* the people within the organisation feel as if they are part of one whole, rather than a fragmented group of individuals who share little in common. Thus, for the

organisation to work, there must be:

• An effort to make all the goals KNOWN and accessible to every individual member

• An effort to involve every individual in the decision-making processes, to give a sense of belonging

• A culture of reward established, which is based as much on effort as achievement

• Ensure that individual contributions are swiftly recognised and rewarded accordingly. Remembering that reward can be praise and recognition, which are as important as monetary gain.

• Give each individual a niche into which he can fit, and where his contribution can be acknowledged

Organisations must foster good communication. Feelings of betrayal and distrust are sensitive issues that require sensitive handling. Without proper channels of communication, and in the hands of managers with low interpersonal skills, small niggles grow quickly to unmanageable proportions and can create fierce opposition to any new ideas that may be in the pipeline.

An organisation must give the overall picture to the employees: what it is doing, why it is doing it, what it is attempting to achieve, how it will achieve it, and most importantly, the particular person's role in the overall process. By encouraging the employees to feel a part of the fabric of the organisation, by giving them a chance to participate and voice opinions, by allowing them to take part in shaping their own destiny, employees will gradually come to understand and become attached to company policy, because they will have been instrumental in formulating it.

The Kaizen pyramid illustrated overleaf is an idea for imbueing an organisation with the correct procedures to achieve and establish a programme for continuous improvement. The pinnacle of success will have been attained when Kaizen is practised throughout the company: the groundwork is the building blocks upon which that pinnacle rests, namely, good labour-management relations; a sense of belonging and purpose; achievable goals and targets; reward and recognition; a long-term view; and visibility.

THE ORGANISATIONAL PYRAMID

Long-termism and visibility

Two of the dimensions along which an organisation needs to travel in order to achieve continuous improvement are long-term strategy and visibility of processes. Too many companies in the West are firefighting - solving daily crises which treat the symptoms but not the disease, rather like patching a plaster over a bleeding wound.

Mention long-term strategy, and an image of the two-to-five year thinker emerges. Mention long-term to a successful Japanese firm and inevitably the targets are geared towards 25-year periods. But they are not alone - the better European strategists like Volvo have also set their sights on where they would like to be twenty-five years from now!

COMPARISON OF LONG-TERM AGAINST SHORT-TERM STRATEGY

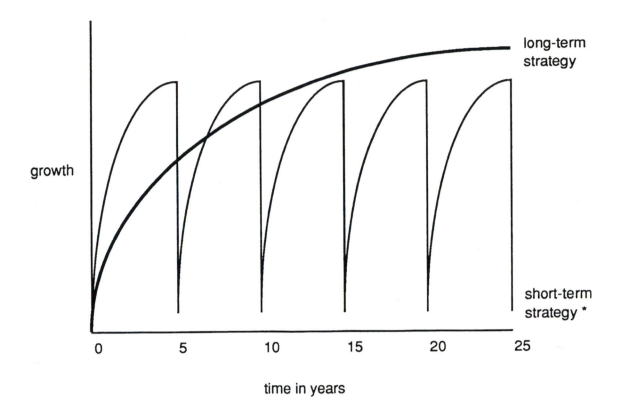

* Assuming the same rate of growth is maintained over the 25-year period

Thinking in the relative future gears a company towards looking for ways in which it must change or adapt in order to survive. Too often short-termism and the lure of financial rewards blinds the company towards the viability of its product within the marketplace of the future. Even if the product was fine, obsolete management practices would endanger the company anyway, and it would still go out of business. Many are the tales of woe of a company which has built its reputation on one item alone, failed to develop and diversify, and has subsequently gone under as a result.

Why must business processes be visible? The answer is that if the people managing the company do not know WHAT the business is about, *from end to end,* then they cannot go about changing it for the better. Visibility allows:

• problems to be seen and discussed, which may have otherwise remained hidden

• responsibility and allocation of problems to be delegated

• conversely, it allows management to see what is being done *right* and then to

24

see if these processes can be adopted elsewhere in the company

• the exercise of control. If management knows what is going wrong and the reasons behind it, then it is far better able to discover ways in which these can be overcome

• the introduction of flexibility into work practices

Finally, for strategic decisions, organisations need to base their assumptions on data. The importance of data collection - its relevance, its truthfulness, its validity - all need to be closely examined if the data is to prove beneficial. Using the wrong data, or analysing it wrongly, simply leads an organisation into making expensive mistakes, which could ultimately affect the viability of the company. Visibility of data allows goals and targets to be set, as well as monitoring progress.

At the managerial level

Cross-functional management

Cross-functional management aims to create a less hierarchical system - it involves both horizontal layers as well as the more traditional vertical approach. The benefits are:

• divisional barriers are broken down, so that dialogue is free-flowing between departments

• communication channels are opened up across the whole organisation so grievances can be readily tackled at the embryo stage

• information can be disseminated to a wider audience

• there is more participation in joint ventures

• each department does not function in isolation to others

• design and manufacture are more closely related, producing a better-conforming product (to the specifications).

TRADITIONAL HIERARCHICAL MANAGEMENT

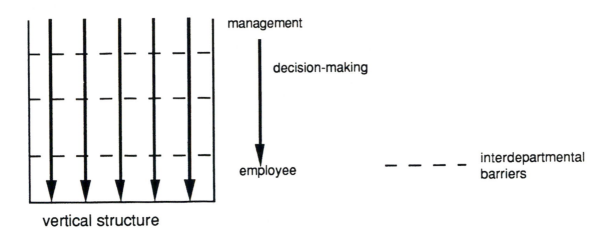

vertical structure

CROSS-FUNCTIONAL MANAGEMENT

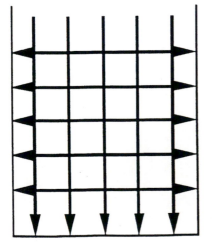

horizontal and vertical hierarchy gives strength
to the fabric of the organisation as it represents the warp and
the weft of decision-making

Cross-functional management means that all the departments are working towards one common goal, rather than just striving for their individual ones. Thus the achievement goes beyond the individual to the corporate goal - that of delivering on time and to budget and to a prerequisite quality. Networking is encouraged as greater liaison between the departments means that the 'user-supplier' relationship is fine-tuned.

Goal-sharing

One of the outcomes of cross-functional management is that there is universal goal-sharing in the company - everyone is aiming for the same endpoint, thus reducing conflicts of interest for that company.

Management is the usual provider for goals (although if it is really Kaizen-conscious, then a substantial part of those goals could be through employee initiatives and consensus) and strategies for achieving those goals. Japanese managers spend up to fifty per cent of their time on improvement projects (M.Imai, 1986) requiring a range of problem-solving techniques from the simple to the sophisticated statistical tools. Subliminal to all improvement efforts is that management should become waste-conscious, firstly because it does not cost anything, and secondly because the potential benefits are manifold.

Managers focus on systems and procedures to shape gradual and on-going *visible* improvement. Goals are set so that they are ambitious but not unattainable. This is aimed to keep the workforce on its toes and prevent a slackening of effort.

The other function of goal-sharing is that concerned with planning and control. It allows for the timely dissemination of collated information to the relevant parties, and for enlightened leadership where each individual's efforts are co-ordinated for the benefit of the company.

Teamwork and bottom-up management

The advantage of group work is that of the "hundred-brain" theory: or to put it in more colloquial terms, two heads are better than one. The collective thinking power of a group of people has to be better than the sum of its parts and is an inherent part of Kaizen philosophy.

A team can foster better the ideology of quality and continuous improvement - when one member falls down, the others can act to bolster his commitment.

Sharing ideas promotes better communication and increased morale. Since there is also an air of informality to this approach to problem-solving, it is non-confrontational in terms of labour-management relations and more time can be spent in developing skills rather than fighting change.

Bottom-up management means spending time with employees to consider their views, collate their disagreements, then eventually reach consensus as to what tasks should be undertaken. The amount of time taken by this route is often tediously long to Western eyes, but the end result is that there is greater ownership of the final decision, because of the prior consultations. Hence, even difficult items are pushed through without worrying that interference is going

to occur at a later stage.

Compare this slow and painstaking build-up of confidence in the Japanese manager to the methods employed by the Western manager - rapid decisions are taken without consensus from employees. If these are unfavourable, then an equal amount of time is spent trying to push it through against an unco-operative workforce. Perhaps the task does get done, but at what cost? Resentful, rebellious staff, low morale, and increasing alienation from the company.

The diagram below represents how a workforce should co-exist in harmony between the various sections (management and other staff) in order to provide a better service to the customer. It includes both the top-down and the bottom-up features of Kaizen, and shows the important areas where management needs to concentrate its effort.

CROSS-FUNCTIONAL MANAGEMENT
Top-down + bottom-up = KAIZEN

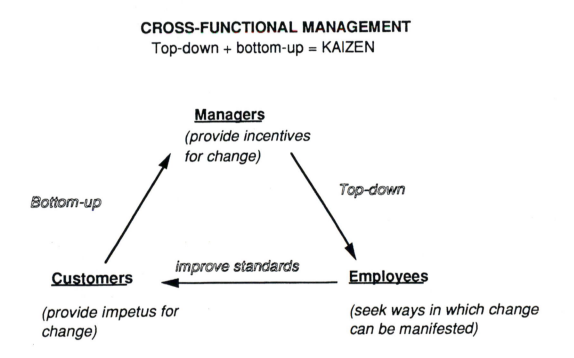

At the individual level

Management's efforts towards the individual should be a nurturing role. Of all the important items in the Kaizen equation, unequivocally the most important is PEOPLE, the individual. Without the co-operation of the individual, all attempts at introducing Kaizen into the company will be doomed to failure.

In order to instil commitment into the employee, both toward his work and the institution which provides it, a mutually symbiotic relationship has to be fostered. The chief ingredient to make this relationship prosper must focus on the motivation of the individual.

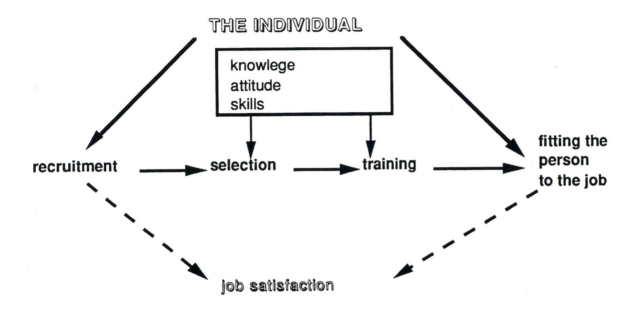

Motivation

Motivation is central to the understanding of the employee, in evaluating his relationship to his job, and also his potential in accomplishing that job to a satisfactory level. Motivation or *Need* theories centre around Maslow, Herzberg and McLelland and all focus upon changing the attitude of the employee to his work. If the employee does not enjoy his work, or divorces it from the rest of his life as a necessary evil, then the potential for improvement is lost.

However, when management decides to hand back **control** of the employee **to** the employee, then motivation becomes a key factor towards improvement.

The employee is:

• empowered
• entrusted
• made to feel that his contributions are worthwhile
• allowed to use his brain as well as his physical strength
• encouraged to adopt a positive attitude to work

• able to enjoy his work due to the power of autonomy

Motivation is aimed at changing the behaviour of employees to become pro-active, thinking, decision-making, responsive members of the organisation. It aims to boost morale and restore the joy in work that is so manifestly lacking across the whole sphere of industry today. When one considers that the average person spends such a large proportion of his life at the workplace, the importance of creating a benevolent atmosphere which encourages participation cannot be overemphasised. And of course, chief amongst the gainers is the company itself.

Task significance

Task significance is where the actual work that the employee is engaged in is related to the overall product or the scheme of things, where the product is not tangible. If the employee is made aware of the importance of what he is doing, if there is visible evidence that the tasks contribute to the good of the whole, then it becomes more satisfying in context, and the employee has an achievable goal.

In recent years this move towards task identity and task significance has been given greater credibility, by allowing the employee to take a task through to completion. Thus instead of doing repetitive work in soldering together parts of a toaster, for example, he is allowed to complete the toaster or a substantial part of it. This allows for a sense of achievement, a visible proof that he has created something, and also aids in teaching skill variety, rather than using one monotonous skill. Variations on this theme have also been adopted across assembly lines such as automobile production.

INTERNAL MOTIVATORS

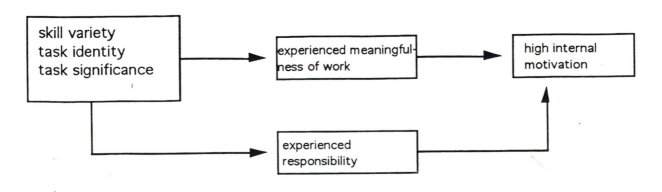

30

Task significance, together with skill variety and task identity, all contribute towards a state of high internal motivation. This is derived from an experienced meaningfulness of the work and an assumption of responsibility for it. When good performance becomes an occasion for self-reward, employees will try to work harder to maintain that sense of achievement.

The fear of failure is removed, but not only that. Because of a wider skills base, the employee has less fear of being unemployed or unemployable, leading to feelings of greater job security. Stable employment is a positive psychological boost for any individual, but it also reflects on the employer. Given the stability of a workforce, the employer is much more likely to invest in future training, which again is one of the fundamental tenets of continuous improvement.

Job satisfaction

If one were to summarise the motive for focusing Kaizen on the individual, it would be INVOLVEMENT. The implication for job involvement, as suggested by several psychologists is that it affects absenteeism - there is a significant negative correlation.

Involvement and participation are affected by job satisfaction, which in itself acts as a motivator in the cycle for continuous improvement. It provides the sustenance when things go wrong, and also as the incentive to continue when ideas peter out.

On the following page is a diagram of some of the factors which influence job satisfaction, both positively and negatively.

On the positive side, satisfaction can help reduce turnover and absenteeism by allowing a person to become committed to his job. Productivity and performance will rise as a consequence, although this is slightly attenuated by age.

On the negative side, low satisfaction will entail the need to redesign the job, so that satisfying elements within it are increased.

Other moderators are the mood of the person, his personality, and job enrichment. The former two cannot be manipulated to any worthwhile predictors, but jobs can be enhanced to provide satisfaction along a range of factors.

For instance:
- setting achievable goals
- knowing the result of one's work endeavours
- having one's ability tested

can contribute to the overall aim. Practical example by the Japanese relates to the provision of overhead computer screens which indicate the targets and current performance levels. Employees have only to look up to see how well (or badly) they are doing. In itself, this is a small thing, but it is a good illustration of the principle.

JOB SATISFACTION AND SOME OF THE POSITIVE AND NEGATIVE INDICATORS OF IT

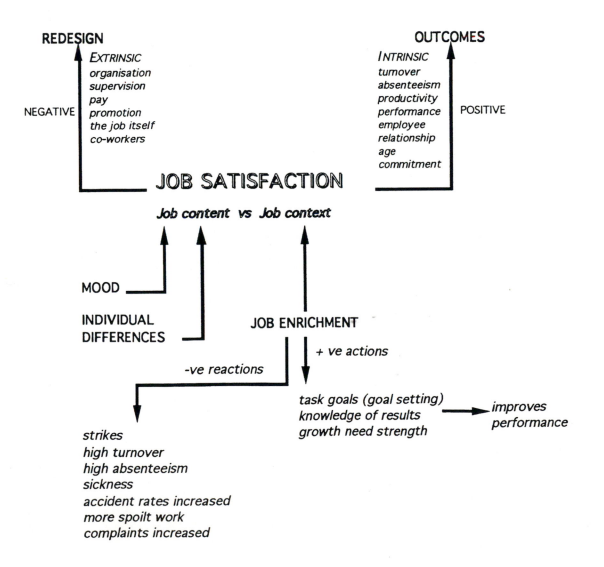

Reward and recognition

According to King (1970), Herzberg's two-factor theory of satisfaction reveals that intrinsic motivators such as:

• achievement

• recognition

• the work itself

• responsibility

• and advancement

all act together to determine job satisfaction.

Job dissatisfaction hinges around:

• company policy
• supervision
• interpersonal relationships with co-workers
• working conditions

Cullen & Hollingum (1987) examined the motivators and found a substantial difference in the duration of satisfaction which they afforded. Responsibility was the longest lasting in effect, followed by the work itself, then advancement. Achievement in financial terms can therefore be interpreted as only a short-term motivator, where the other factors are present.

However, the opposite of this is that when none of the motivators are present, then reward (in monetary terms) becomes of vital importance because it acts as a focal point for the dissatisfaction with the job.

Put in simple terms, man does not work for bread alone - if he is happy in his employment, he may still work well, because of other compensatory factors. Remove the compensations and his perceptions become distorted.

Reward which is considered valuable is praise. It has been proved that people work better and for longer given adequate praise for their efforts, and that this is the most potent long-term motivator of all.

Training

The beginning and the end of continuous improvement is training.
The beginning of the end is lack of training.

On-the-job training, off-the-job training, and independent study are the basic tenets for uniformly raising the consciousness of the worker. Training should always be given as a priority, starting at the top of the company, so that Kaizen projects not only enjoy a high profile, but so that such a high level initiative ensures that decision-makers are actively involved to implement whatever changes are deemed necessary for the success of the programme.

Training should be a continuous exercise, with a bent towards learning new methods and techniques, whilst forever trying to improve on the old ones. Training broadens knowledge and deepens understanding, such that the robotic nature of a production line can be transformed in perception, to an opportunity for creative problem-solving.

This removes the drudgery of routine work and allows flexibility both within and across the workforce. New product development ensues naturally from this process, and is a challenging new perspective for an employee, as it gives him direction, and his work meaning.

Groupism and stealing jobs

As suggested before, groupism is a way of life for the Japanese. It is more difficult for a Western worker to participate as a team member than as an individual. But it is by no means impossible. Human beings by their very nature are social animals, they prefer to be in groups, they work better as a group, their loyalties are enhanced because of group membership. And that applies as much to the local streetgang as it does to members of a management board.

So perhaps it is now time to rethink the approach to work that has been conditioned into us since primary school - ME, MY TERRITORY should give way to the "US" way of thinking.

How simple it would be to humanise work; to encourage people to work together and exercise these dormant needs for companionship. A fundamental change of attitude to the way in which work is conducted needs to be initiated. Employees should be assigned tasks as groups, with each person having his own responsibilities, but also being responsible to the group overall. If in doubt

how to proceed, clearly one should begin by asking the employee how he would best like to work. One could say many things about such a tactical manoevre. Radical ? Yes ! Terrifying ? Yes ! Impossible ? Definitely not !!

Often the most difficult people to convince are the managers. They think that decentralising power and responsibility undermines their position and creates instability. Yet they fail to see that spending time on irrelevancies which can be more easily dealt with by people at the heart of the problem, diminishes their time and their effort from the real job: *managing*.

Indeed managers are sometimes the most potent barriers to success in a Kaizen *programme.*

Scepticism on the part of managers, or fear, or impatience with long-term goals do not help the concept, which is essentially about changing attitudes. Barrie Dale of UMIST* found that in 35 out of the 132 manufacturing companies that he surveyed regarding management attitude to change, nine types of objection were raised, showing that if managers remain unconvinced or feel threatened, then they will try to prove a scheme unsuccessful, discreetly or otherwise.

Finally, we turn to the question of stealing jobs. Western jobs are very rigid in their description: there are precise dos and dont's and the territoriality of jobs is finely demarcated and vigorously defended. It is unthinkable for one person to encroach on another's job.

In Japan, usually the reverse occurs. There is a huge grey area of job definition. Allocation of jobs is not needed - when an employee is free and perceives a backlog, he will attend to it regardless. It is not thought of as incompetency on anyone's part; the aim is to maintain output, and workers help each other out as and when necessary. The only prerequisite is that the worker must have achieved competency in the task.

This is a much more humane and satisfactory way of dealing with workflow: rather than overburdening one party, the allocation of responsibilty is to the group, and group members share equally in the race to meet quotas.

Since job delineation is less rigorous, the other benefit is of skill-sharing. Due to the stability of the system, the employee does not feel vulnerable to job insecurity, thus he is more willing to share his knowledge with other members of the group. Learning is open to all, and becomes a vehicle for continuous improvement.

* UMIST= University of Manchester Institute of Science and Technology

Chapter Four

MAN, MACHINES, METHODS, MATERIALS, MEASUREMENT

Kaizen cannot be practised in isolation. Neither can it be practised piecemeal. The total equation must take into consideration each aspect of the process. These include:

• Manpower

• The machines involved in the process

• The methods used in the process

• The materials used in the process

• The measurement of the process to see where it conforms to requirements

By examining each of these facets in turn, waste in all its various forms can be identified and gradually eliminated. The process can be honed to deliver exactly according to and above specification. And discipline will regulate the workplace, because things will have been put in order, with a place for everything and everything in its place. In other words good housekeeping and common sense with a fancy name.

THE FOUR M'S

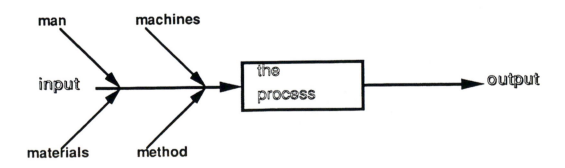

Using the structure of the four M's as a way of initiating Kaizen means that nothing is left out of, or overlooked in, the analysis of the process. This ensures that there is less likelihood of causing error in the search for

improvement.

The next step following on from looking at the four M's is to use the 5W1H method of problem-investigation. The 5W1H represents the who, what, where, why, when, and how method of problem assessment which systematically examines each aspect of a problem for causality. They will be discussed in the next section.

Who? What? Where? When? Why? How?

Having defined the areas upon which to concentrate, the above questions should be asked for each of them. Thus for Manpower, questions which could arise are:

• Who is doing the job

• Who else is doing it

• Who should be doing the job

• Who else could be doing it

• Who is able to do the job

This ties in with the earlier discussion of fitting the person to the job - finding the person who is most competent at it; and if there is no-one available, then using this as a basis for a training programme - matching the skills to be taught to the requirements of the job.

The other questions determine what the person does, where he does it, when he does it, why he does it, and how he does it.

In this method nothing is too small or too irrelevant to be ignored. By looking attentively at the many trivial causes which constitute a problem, a major factor may be uncovered which has later implications for the process.

37

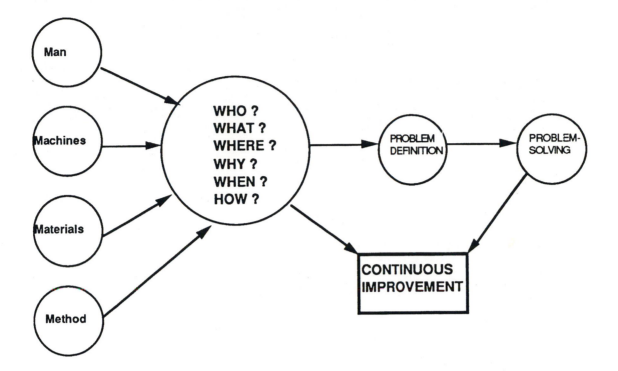

Each of the 4M's is then taken through an in-depth analysis to reveal responsibilities, requirements, presence of standards, any unusual or unexplained features, capabilities for meeting system requirements, layout, consistency, breakdowns (how many and how often), mistakes, adequacy of methods used. The list is endless. It must be comprehensive.

When everything has been taken in to account, then task forces are designated to try and tackle some of the more pressing problems. This is where the mechanism of suggestion systems can come into play.

Suggestion schemes

Suggestion schemes can range from the ubiquitously simple cardboard box, to sophisticated techniques for collating and assessing employee ideas. Toyota's suggestion scheme, for example, reached 1,900,000 in the 1980's, 95% of which were implemented. This was an average of 32 suggestions per employee per year.

Naturally, the success of Toyota, and to a lesser degree other companies who have a strong suggestion scheme in action, begs the question 'Why does it not succeed here?'

Suggestion schemes, like all other aspects of Kaizen, are highly dependent on management to carry them through. Without visible commitment, without a sense of management participation, inevitably the strongest desire to improve will gradually weaken and fade. Crucial to the operation and survival of such a scheme, therefore, must be an awareness and commitment towards what is being attempted; meticulous planning must occur for the inauguration of the scheme and then monitoring and recognition for the ideas that filter through.

MANAGEMENT'S ROLE FOR SUGGESTION SCHEME SUCCESS

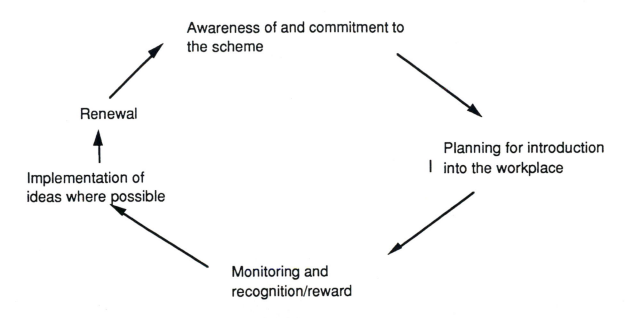

Prejudice or bias will seriously impede success, as will lack of responsiveness. The author is aware of one company which encourages participation in the scheme by implementing the suggestion within the next working day, if it does not do any harm and is small enough not to require lengthy discussion. The philosophy behind this is that, as long as the suggestion is not harmful, it will show the employee that he is being treated seriously, and that further suggestions which emanate from him could prove beneficial at a later date. The foundations are laid to invest for the long-term and make the scheme self-perpetuating.

Furthermore, the perception of reward is immediate. Since the employee sees his suggestion being implemented without delay, he is made aware of the importance of the role that the scheme plays in continuous improvement. This can prove to be as potent as monetary reward, although the latter is no doubt welcome!

Quality circles

One of the most effective ways of introducing teamwork and group involvement is the use of quality circles within the work programme. Quality circles are voluntary groups of people who can be either intra- or inter-departmental, who meet informally or otherwise to discuss the 'trivial many problems' incurred during every day work practices and suggest areas for improvement. In keeping with the Kaizen philosophy, these are small, incremental, gradual improvements which alone can be considered as insignificant, but over a period of time their value is considerable.

The emphasis for quality circles is in group working. The benefits derived are:

• All workers are helped to achieve the same level of understanding of the problem

• Weaker members of the group are not isolated but encouraged and helped to learn by other team members

• The supervisor provides a direct link for information flow to higher levels of management

• Feedback for ideas is available, also the possibility of the idea being incorporated gives the incentive to think up new ones.

• Creative thinking is not confined to a chosen few, who are removed from the realities of the workplace

• People who form the backbone of the organisation are the ones most able to pinpoint problems

• Cross-fertilisation of ideas contributes to the company's health.

According to Lillrank and Noriaki, the proper function of the quality circle is workshop maintenance and improvements through groupwork. One would consider the first part of the statement to be rather limiting - for quality circles are applicable to use wherever there are problems, and problems certainly do **not** confine themselves to only one part of an organisation.

WHY WHITE COLLAR CIRCLES FAILED

REASONS FOR FAILURE	PERCENTAGE
Immediate supervisor's attitude	57
Lack of projects	44
Staff movement	40
Leader's lack of time	40
Redundancies/economic situation/ disillusionment	34

(Source: adapted from R. Collard, 1989)

To facilitate the work of quality circles, several principles and tools are applied. These are the PDCA cycle, the Seven statistical tools for data collection and analysis, and the QC (Quality Circle) story.

Quality circles are to some extent a motivational concept. A high desire to succeed, multiplied by a low expectation of succeeding, leads to low effort. To counteract this low effort, management must be seen to be be supportive at all times. It must help in the initial establishment of a quality circle environment by introducing the ideas of teamwork and problem-solving; subsequently, by providing the right sort of backup through provision of training in problem-solving techniques. A good training programme lays the essential groundwork necessary for momentum to be maintained during episodes when difficulties arise.

To further the understanding of the quality circle members, and also to provide initial advisors, a co-ordinator and a facilitator should be present.

They can help regulate meetings, and provide a structured and systematic approach to agendas and timescales. However, the facilitator must also be trained, not least in human resource management, including the psychology of

41

groupworking, which is an important aspect of the schedule.

Role of the Co-ordinator

1. Generates enthusiasm for the promotion of the QC

2. Administrative duties including time management

3. Communication channel between different QCs

4. Link for information to naive parties i.e.,
those not involved in the circle

5. Provides access to top management, therefore
must have senior position in the company

Role of the facilitator

1. Usually drawn from middle management, but role
is more temporary that the co-ordinator

2.Feedback and nurturing capacity to supervisor
of the QC

3.Vital for establishing the circle

Role of the circle leader

1. Usually the supervisor or foreman

2. Leadership to teach group self-sufficiency

3. Knowledge of systematic problem-solving to be disseminated to group members

4. Put members at ease with each other

5. Remove elitist stigma from the eyes of non-participants; show that group is non-threatening to them

6. Show realities of the situation, so that wild expectations are not made by anyone

7. Encourage where progress is slow

8. Keep projects within definable objectives

9. Teach the art of presentation to management

Presentation and publicity

This is an important aspect of the quality circle activity and is given at the end of each problem after data has been collated and analysed and solutions offered. It is an opportunity for management to judge for itself the advantages of allowing employees to use their initiative and expertise and give recognition to it. At the same time there is wider recognition for the quality circle activity throughout the company, fostering awareness and interest.

Training for the presentation is vital because of the implied weight behind the message. Presenters and managers need to be able to communicate to sell their ideas, in the same language of management, because the latter are under no obligation to accept any of the recommendations made.

Data collection

The basis for quality circle work lies in objective data collection, which is then used as a method for judging the validity of a project. This is a very sound approach with which to tackle problems, because there are no personalities involved. The simplest tools available are the seven statistical tools and these comprise:

Graphs
Histograms
Pareto Charts
Checksheets
Scatter Diagrams
Control Charts
Cause-and-Effect-Diagrams

Added to these are the New Seven, which are:

Relations Diagram
Affinity Diagram
Tree Diagram
Matrix Diagram
Matrix Data-analysis Diagram
Process Decision Program Chart
Arrow Diagram

The New Seven will not be considered here as strictly speaking they are not fundamental to a Kaizen programme. However, the old Seven (also known as Q7), are indispensable and elementary enough for solving up to 95 % of all the problems within a company.

Graphs

Graphs are a simple way of representing data pictorially. They act as a visual aid in remembering and assimilating complex information, and can be used to convey trends, patterns and relationships which would otherwise be difficult to interpret from figures alone.

Types of graphs include:
Bar graphs
Line Graphs
Pie charts
Band graphs

Gantt charts

The most commonly used types of graph are bar, pie and line. All these graphs are best at presenting overviews rather than minutae of detail. Examples are shown below.

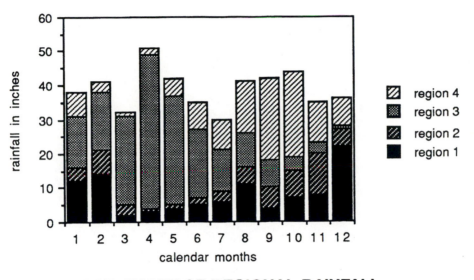

A BAR CHART OF REGIONAL RAINFALL

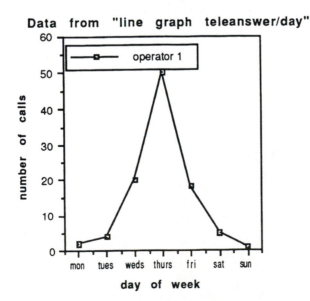

A LINE GRAPH SHOWING THE NUMBER OF CALLS PER DAY

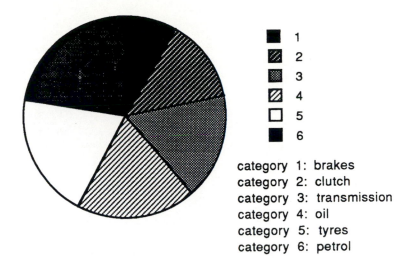

category 1: brakes
category 2: clutch
category 3: transmission
category 4: oil
category 5: tyres
category 6: petrol

A PIE CHART OF CAR FAILURES IN ONE MONTH IN CATEGORIES 1-6 (For the servicing records of a garage)

Histograms

Histograms are used to represent frequency distributions, for instance age, income, sales. They are a form of bar graph that provide information on the distribution of observations, as well as quantities and their relationship. Histograms can show:

(a) shape
(b) typical value
(c) overall spread
(d) any quantity out of tolerance limits

The basic difference between a histogram and a bar graph, is that in a histogram it is the area of each block which represents the frequency of a group, but in a bar graph it is the HEIGHT of the block which is representative. Histograms of less than 25 points are unlikely to reveal relevant information. Typical examples of where histograms can prove valuable information are:

• to chart the accuracy of machines

• to study process performance

46

• to identify and eliminate defects

• to improve yield quality

• to compare the output of a process with its requirements

**HISTOGRAM OF HOUSE PRICES (IN 1000'S)
AGAINST % OF HOUSES IN THE AREA**

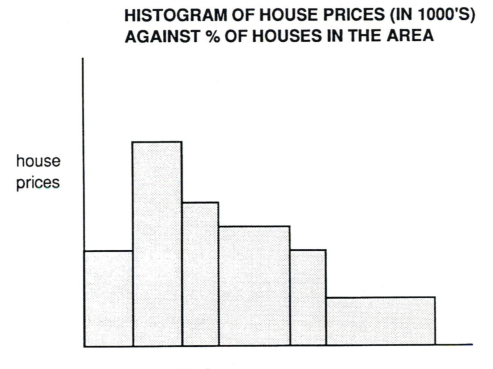

In a histogram, the distribution of the data will point out small variations which may not have been readily apparent. One other thing to note is that there are no gaps between the bars of the histogram as there are in bar graphs.

Pareto analysis

Juran noted that the vital few data elements accounted for most of the total effect in any situation, and that conversely, the bulk of data elements accounted for very little of the total effect. This phenomenon is known as the Pareto principle and can also be called the 80/20 rule.

Juran limited his observations to manufacturing and engineering, but the rule is universal in its application. Thus problems can be identified by brainstorming - which is a technique where a group of people bounce as many ideas as they can

off each other. None is discarded until each is discussed in turn for its relative merits.

All the most important ideas are then discussed thoroughly until consensus is reached as to the most appropriate one to tackle. If the problems are drawn onto a graph, then a curve will indicate the vital few which are causing the maximum nuisance.

A point to note: the 80/20 ratio is not hard and fast in its application: it could be 70/30 or 60/40 for instance, but the principle remains the same.

THE PARETO PRINCIPLE

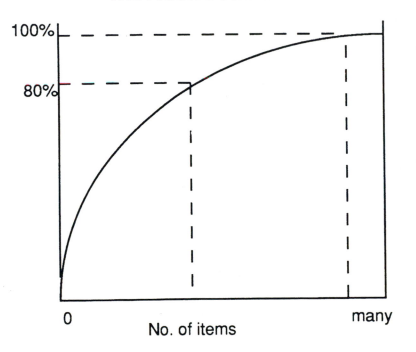

Checksheets

A checksheet is a tool for collecting various items of data in an orderly manner. The format allows a clear and easily interpretable form. There are two types of checksheet: a recording checksheet and a location checksheet.

A recording checksheet

This is to both collect and organise data. The marks in the tabulation column correspond to a graphical representation of the data even before an analysis has occurred.

A location checksheet

This is used to identify physical locations. For example, to identify defects in the paintwork on a car there will be a diagram of the car with points marked on it where the paint has failed to be sprayed. This way both the frequency and the position of the defect can be recorded.

The usual way in which data is recorded is in the form of five-bar gates: that is four vertical strokes with the fifth stroke cutting diagonally through them. Once the data for the checksheet has been collected, the totals for each horizontal row and vertical column are calculated, and this in turn is used to pinpoint certain areas for attention. Furthermore, the range, the minimum and the maximum values can also be obtained at a glance.

CHECKSHEET OF DEFECTS IN ON-TIME DELIVERY OF GOODS

time	mon	tues	weds	thurs	fri	total
9am	1111	11	111		1111	15
12 noon						
2pm	1					
4pm	111					
total	9					

Checksheets can also be used as follow-ups to the improvement event and to ensure that there has actually been an upturn in the results as a consequence.

Scatter diagrams

Scattergrams are used to examine the relationship between two factors to see if a correlation exists. If they are related, then by controlling the independent factor, the dependent factor will also be controlled. The type of relationship can be determined by the scattering of the points on the diagram. If these are dispersed, then there is no relationship, whereas if the points are close together, then some relationship can be ascertained. A perfect relationship is exhibited by a straight line of points.

Scattergrams have application in problem-solving following cause-and-effect analysis.

A SCATTER DIAGRAM SHOWING RELATIONSHIP LINE OF BEST FIT

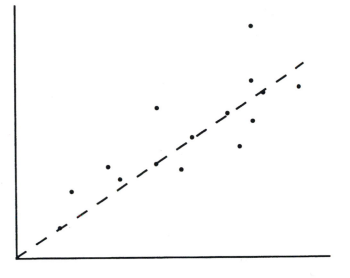

Cause-and-effect Diagrams

An essential feature of cause-and-effect analysis is again brainstorming. Basically what happens is that a problem is identified by brainstorming, or even by Pareto, and is listed on the right hand side of the page at the point of the arrow. Lines emanate radially from this central arrow, and are the causes of that particular problem. Classification under the headings of *man, machines, materials and method* will help to reveal sub-causes, until precise detail is reached. The other names for this tool are the 'fishbone' or 'Ishikawa' diagram.

Cause-and-effect is useful for both identifying problems and for finding ways in which good results can be achieved. Thus the latter are left less to chance and are dependent instead on changing the process in a knowledgeable way.

LAYOUT FOR A CAUSE-EFFECT DIAGRAM

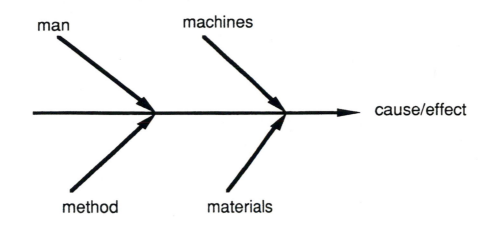

Statistical process control

There is inherent variability within every process. However by controlling this variability through visual means, an acceptable range can be worked out. Oakland has found that even in 100% inspection at least 15% of defectives present are missed due to task repetitiveness or monotony.

Control charts are devices for setting upper and lower limits of acceptability of the process under review. They are no more than a graphical representation of data over time, but the method is very powerful for regulating the process, since new data can be compared to previous performance.

The purpose of the control chart is to distinguish between natural variations and variations due to assignable causes such as tiredness, lack of concentration, machine failure etc.

Chapter Five

WHAT ARE THE COSTS?

The greatest cost of Kaizen is in **TIME**. Time is needed for all the different ideas outlined to be explained, and to be adopted, then to establish these as normal practice in the workplace. Time is needed for management to teach itself and then to sell the idea of continuous improvement to its employees.

Just as a mighty oak takes time to grow from a humble acorn, so do the seeds of Kaizen need to be sown and watered, then developed to their full potential. A Kaizen programme must not have definable time limits set on it from the beginning. Growth is insidious, but obstacles may be many and varied in the path to total acceptance.

Yet most managers will argue that time is too valuable to be spent frivolously on such soft issues as humanity in work, on returning to basic values of workmanship. Resources are scarce and expenditure on investments such as training are neglected at the expense of chasing that mercurial bottom-line. Recession has bitten hard and deep worldwide in recent years and pruning the workforce has been mandatory across a wide range of industries. Thus the most valuable resource of these companies is being squandered away, when they are in essence, the means for survival (and also revival).

The other cost of Kaizen is **commitment**. Without the drive, the ambition to *want* to improve, any effort will ultimately become half-hearted. People must be shown the benefits that can be derived from the Kaizen way of thinking by putting it in sharp juxtaposition to the practices currently in vogue.

The potential costs of not using Kaizen are varied and far-reaching. They affect such internal aspects of job failure as rework, to external ones connected to repair and warranty claims; the useless expenditure on inspections and audits which still fail to ensure quality at the *beginning of the manufacturing process, not at the end of it;* the use of unqualified personnel through lack of training. Some of these costs are illustrated in the diagram below.

THE POTENTIAL COSTS OF NOT USING KAIZEN

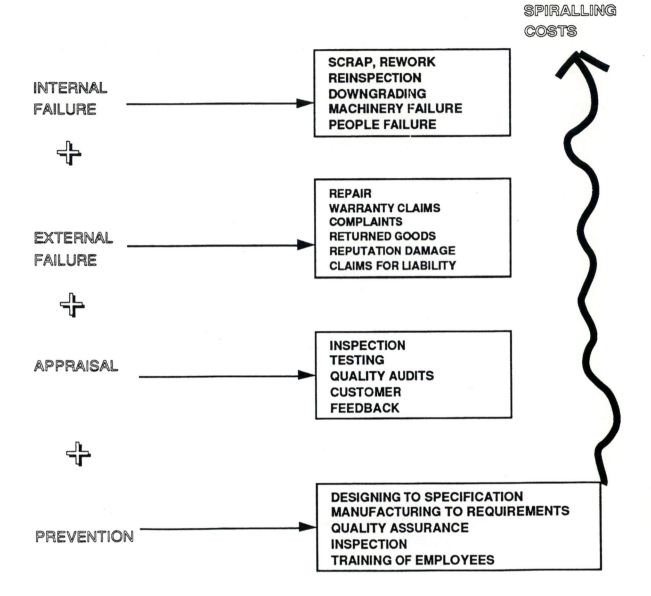

The Advantages and Disadvantages of Using Kaizen

The advantages

Kaizen can be useful in any industry, whether it is ailing or not. What are the advantages of using it?

• First and foremost *it puts people first*

53

• It concentrates attention on the processes and activity is centred on getting the process right

• It rewards effort as well as achievement

• The 'bottom-line' does not become the primary reason for a company to set strategic targets

• It is a method for active problem-solving

• It delegates responsibility to all participants

• It gives employees a sense of purpose

• It acts as a motivator for building quality into a product

• It eliminates the need for inspection

• It harbours group-centred activity and therefore encourages teamwork

• It helps to breakdown departmental barriers

• The focus for improvement is returned to the needs of the customer

• It aims to reduce waste and superfluous activity which are non-value-adding to the company

• It reduces the costs of operation by making the reasons for high costs visible to management

• It helps to establish long-term goals for the company, so that it can keep abreast of change

These are only some of the more obvious reasons for starting down the path to continuous improvement. The list is limited only by the imagination of the observer. In any activity, there is endless opportunity to do things better, then to do better again. By adopting the philosophy whole-heartedly, people can be inspired to achieve levels of quality and craftsmanship hitherto thought impossible. The human mind is limitless in its ability to achieve. All that is required is a believing heart, and a strong will. The desire to improve, once caught, will be self-perpetuating when the benefits of that improvement become visible. People must believe in themselves and their ability to do better. Of course it is frightening to change, to break out of a humdrum state of

affairs. But if one does not try, the chances are that the rut merely grows deeper and more difficult to get out of.

The disadvantages

Kaizen is not a new idea - it has been in practice, both in parts and in toto for a good many years now. But the West is still shy of exploiting it to its full potential. Some of the reasons why this is so are:

• The difficulties in getting started. Just where *does* one start? *(My unequivocal answer to that would be with management!)*

• The difficulties in understanding the concept as a whole from a Western point of view

• Changing people's attitude to accept something different and by implication *foreign (the answer to that again would be to remove the foreignness by emphasising the points of similarity. Human beings are similar enough in the most basic elements wherever they happen to live)*

• Maintaining momentum once the initial fizz has gone out of the proceedings. All too often, introductions are gimmicky and full of razzamattaz, but they fail to have substance and therefore inevitably fail.

• Getting people to think in the long-term

• Trying to convince people that quality is not costly, but actually SAVES money and time and effort.

• Getting away from the 'inspection' culture, which admits to failure even before it has occurred

• Diehard managerial practice which thrives on territoriality and the big-brother syndrome

• The time investment of starting and keeping going any continuous improvement initiative. People are desperate about time, but how effectively is it managed?

• Too much involvement needed from management. It *is* hard work, but managers work hard already. They are just not working on the right things, that's all!

"Which one particular feature of Kaizen should I adopt?"

At the beginning of this management report, I represented Kaizen as a sunburst. Thus the concentrated effect of Kaizen is felt through myriad rays of improvement effort which fall in different spheres. Just as one ray of sunshine is indistinguishable and inseparable from the other, so the different components of Kaizen are inseparable. Conversely, the whole is composed of the sum of its parts, and to leave out one thing diminishes that whole. Thus I would say that Kaizen cannot be divided into little bits, some of which can be missed out. To do so would not be true to the idea of gradual, incremental change. It would dilute and belittle the phenomenon.

In my opinion, Kaizen, to work properly, must be an all-or-nothing commitment. Everything must be taken into consideration because every little counts. When one starts to omit single items, one is open to the danger of then omitting substantial elements of the Kaizen principle, regarding them as unnecessary or obsolete. We have travelled down that slippery slope before. It is time to re-think objectives.

There is no one particular feature of Kaizen that works by itself, just as there is no one particular way of addressing a problem within a company. Each individual and each organisation is unique in its problems. Kaizen is simply a series of tried and tested methods for finding solutions to some of the more common. When these have been solved, then they will point the way in which the uniqueness can be addressed. If you throw out some of the tools at the start of your repair job, what are you going to do when you find later that they are part of your diagnostic apparatus ?

56

Will it work for me?

No one recipe will guarantee success. Neither does it doom to failure. Below are a few guidelines for achieving that first crucial step towards Kaizen.

1. Start simple

2. Start small

3. Choose something do-able

4. Choose people who are committed to the project

5. Give it a high profile

6. Give it priority

7. Give it a short timescale

8. Give it a chance - something which has a high probability of success

9. Involve high command

10. Publish and publicise the results (especially internally!)

11. Adopt it as company standard if appropriate

12. Start again on another small project, either with the same group or a different one.

CASE STUDIES

DIAMOND-STAR MOTORS

Diamond-Star is a collaborative effort between Chrysler Motors Corporation and Mitsubishi Motors Corporation, inaugurated in 1970. It is sited at Illinois, USA, and is a state-of-the-art factory incorporating robotics, just-in-time and a smooth production flow system. 240,000 cars were turned out annually in the late 1980s.

The focus for the quality initiative has been on the workers. They work in teams in the manufacturing process and are regularly trained on all aspects of quality. Each person is responsible for a high quality product.

The charm of Diamond-Star is that it is a joint venture, in American territory, for introducing Kaizen to the workplace. The resultant success must provide evidence, therefore, that Kaizen does work in other environments than the Japanese (although to qualify this statement, one must admit that a large number of Japanese personnel were present at the outset of the company.)

Other ways that Diamond-Star have adopted Kaizen are:

• Delegating individual responsibility

• Use of quality circles

• Use of suggestion schemes

• Self-inspection

• The next process is the customer

• Raising standards

• Harmony and teamwork

• Fitting the person to the job and the work environment (i.e., selection). Psychological and personality variables were taken into consideration

• Use of quality tools

• Establishing quality supplier relationships, usually single-source

• Skill variety is taught to each new employee

• Ownership of processes

• Comprehensive information-gathering on quality issues

NISSAN MOTORS

What are the ways in which Nissan is implementing Kaizen?

• The use of Poka-Yoke (mistake-proofing), to lessen the number of rejects

• Concentrating on the customer-supplier relationship, by putting themselves in the supplier's shoes.

• Using PDCA during development

• Standard setting

• Formation of Kaizen teams (similar to quality circles) to focus on improvement issues

• Single-sourcing of suppliers, therefore supplier development

• Concentrating on achieving Kaizen in quality, cost and delivery

THE CANON PRODUCTION SYSTEM

Canon has moved and diversified itself as a company, from producing cameras, to other optical equipment, fax machines, photocopiers and other business requisites in a remarkably short space of time. Dynamic changes in which the production process was overhauled to accommodate new ways of doing things, as well as comprehensive training for Kaizen activity ensures that it will move with the times to remain a competitive organisation. How *did* Canon do it ?

Again the ultimate aim was quality, cost and delivery improvements.

• Waste was identified in all quarters of the production system. It was found in:

1. The manufacturing process (the time taken from raw material to finished product)
2. The production of defects, and associated rework, disposal
3. The waste in equipment - cost effectiveness was not present; inefficiency
4. Waste in expenses: hidden manufacturing costs e.g. light, heat
5. Use of indirect labour i.e., non-value-adding
7. Waste in human resources
8. Waste in operations
9. Waste in start-up

All these areas of waste were measured, monitored, then ways were found for eliminating them. The improvements gained were expressed as percentage profit to give everyone visible evidence for what had been hidden.

Other areas in which Canon concentrated its effort were:

• Motivating the workforce for: self-respect, self-reliance, teamwork

• Lack of discrimination between various sections of the workforce. Demarcation of different types of worker was lifted post-Second World War

• Supporting the worker in the drive for continuous improvement

• Training

• Reward and commitment from top management

• Organizing the continuous flow factory (just-in-time)

• Cost control

Conclusion

As can be seen from the above examples, the use and application of Kaizen is varied. It can work across a diversity of industries as well as a diversity of cultures. It does work, once it has been fully understood and accepted. It requires full participation.

The road to continuous improvement is long and at times bumpy. Many become lost or disillusioned along the way. But examples abound of the firms who have made it, to light the path of followers. It is just a matter of choice. And as Dr Edwards Deming, the guru of total quality so aptly put it , "survival is not compulsory".

References

Kaizen. Masaaki Imai. 1986 The Kaizen Institute

Cullen J & Hollingum J: Implementing Total Quality 1987 IFS Ltd

Ishikawa K: What is Total Quality Control 1985 Prentice-Hall

Lillrank P & Noriaki K: Continuous Improvement 1989

The Canon Production System 1987 Productivity Press

Oakland J S: Total Quality Management 1989 Heinemann

David AJ: the customer/supplier relationship - the Nissan Way
Total Quality Management, Vol 1 No. 1 1990

Parsons JT: Diamond-Star Motors: Quality from the start;
Total Quality Management Nov. 1988

Collard R: Total Quality: Success through people 1989
Institute of Personnel Management